I0866717

Animals That Live on the Farm/
Animales de la granja

Goats/Cabras

By JoAnn Early Macken

Reading Consultant: Jeanne Clidas, Ph.D.
Director, Roberts Wesleyan College Literacy Clinic

Gareth Stevens
PUBLISHING

Please visit our website, www.garethstevens.com.
For a free color catalog of all our high-quality books,
call toll free 1-800-542-2595 or fax 1-877-542-2596.

Library of Congress Cataloging-in-Publication Data

Macken, JoAnn Early, 1953–
[Goats. Spanish & English]
Goats = Cabras / by JoAnn Early Macken.
p. cm.— (Animals that live on the farm = Animales de la granja)
Includes bibliographical references and index.
ISBN-10: 1-4339-2429-3 ISBN-13: 978-1-4339-2429-3 (lib. bdg.)
ISBN-10: 1-4339-2473-0 ISBN-13: 978-1-4339-2473-6 (soft cover)
1. Goats—Juvenile literature. I. Title. II. Title: Cabras.
SF383.35.M2218 2010
636.3′9—dc22 2009011970

This edition first published in 2010 by
Gareth Stevens Publishing
111 East 14th Street, Suite 349
New York, NY 10003

Copyright © 2010 by Gareth Stevens, Inc.

Executive Managing Editor: Lisa M. Herrington
Senior Editor: Barbara Bakowski
Cover Designers: Jennifer Ryder-Talbot and Studio Montage
Production: Studio Montage
Translators: Tatiana Acosta and Guillermo Gutiérrez
Library Consultant: Carl Harvey, Library Media Specialist, Noblesville, Indiana

Photo credits: Cover, pp. 1, 5, 7, 9, 13, 15 Shutterstock; p. 11 © James P. Rowan; p. 17 © Sharon Eide and Elizabeth Flynn/SandEphoto.com; pp. 19, 21 Gregg Andersen

All rights reserved. No part of this book may be reproduced, stored in a retrieval system, or transmitted in any form or by any means, electronic, mechanical, photocopying, recording, or otherwise, without the prior written permission of the copyright holder. For permission, contact **permissions@gspub.com**.

Printed in the United States of America

1 2 3 4 5 6 7 8 9 14 13 12 11 10 09

Table of Contents

Contenido

Boldface words appear in the glossary./
Las palabras en **negrita** aparecen en el glosario.

A Different Kind of Kid

A baby goat is called a **kid**. A kid can stand soon after it is born.

Cabritos

La cría de la cabra es el **cabrito**. Un cabrito puede pararse poco después de nacer.

kid/
cabrito

A kid drinks milk from its mother at first. After a few weeks, it eats hay or grain.

Al principio, el cabrito bebe la leche de su madre. Después de unas semanas, come heno o grano.

Kids play with each other. They leap and climb. They wag their short tails. A goat that is one year old is called a **yearling**.

Los cabritos son muy juguetones. Saltan y trepan. Menean su corta cola. Una cría de un año de edad recibe el nombre de **chivo**.

yearlings/
chivos

Grown-Up Goats

Male and female goats have horns. Many goats also have beards.

Cabras adultas

Tanto los machos como las hembras tienen cuernos. Muchas cabras también tienen barba.

horns/
cuernos
beard/
barba

In warm weather, goats stay outside. They eat plants, roots, nuts, and berries. They nibble grass. A group of goats is called a **herd**.

Cuando hace buen tiempo, las cabras están al aire libre. Comen plantas, raíces, frutos secos y bayas. Mordisquean la hierba. Un grupo de cabras forma un **rebaño**.

herd/
rebaño

In cold or wet weather, goats stay in a barn or shed. They keep out of the rain, snow, and wind.

Cuando hace frío o llueve, las cabras se quedan en un establo o cobertizo. Allí están protegidas de la lluvia, la nieve y el viento.

Work and Play

Some people keep goats as pets. Others use goats to carry loads. A goat may wear a basket over its back or pull a small cart.

Trabajar y jugar

Algunas personas tienen cabras como mascotas. Otras las usan para acarrear cosas. Una cabra puede llevar una cesta en el lomo o arrastrar un pequeño carrito.

Some farmers raise goats for their **wool**. The farmer cuts off the goats' wool so it can be made into yarn.

Algunos granjeros crían cabras por la **lana**. El granjero corta la lana de las cabras para hacer hilo.

wool/
lana

Some farmers raise goats for milk. They milk the goats twice a day.

Algunos granjeros crían cabras por su leche. Ordeñan las cabras dos veces al día.

Fast Facts/Datos básicos

Height/ Altura	about 3 feet (1 meter) at the shoulder/ unos 3 pies (1 metro) en la cruz
Length/ Longitud	about 4 feet (1 meter) nose to tail/ unos 4 pies (1 metro) de nariz a cola
Weight/ Peso	about 120 pounds (54 kilograms)/ unas 120 libras (54 kilogramos)
Diet/ Dieta	grass, plants, nuts, roots, and berries/hierba, plantas, frutos secos, raíces y bayas
Average life span/ Promedio de vida	up to 15 years/ hasta 15 años

Glossary/Glosario

herd: a large group of goats or other animals

kid: a baby goat

wool: a goat's coat

yearling: a goat that is one year old

---

cabrito: cría de la cabra

chivo: cría de la cabra de un año de edad

lana: pelo de la cabra

rebaño: grupo grande de cabras y de otros animales

For More Information/Más información

Books/Libros

Animals at the Farm/Animales de la granja.
English-Spanish Foundations (series). Gladys Rosa-Mendoza (me+mi publishing, 2004)

Goats. Down on the Farm (series). Sally Morgan (Crabtree Publishing, 2008)

Web Sites/Páginas web

Breeds of Goats/Razas de cabras
www.ansi.okstate.edu/breeds/goats
Read about many kinds of goats./Conozcan distintas razas de cabras.

Kids' Farm: Goats/*Kids' Farm:* Cabras
nationalzoo.si.edu/Animals/KidsFarm/InTheBarn/Goats/factsheet.cfm
Meet the goats at the National Zoo Kids' Farm./Conozcan las cabras de la granja del Zoológico Nacional.

Publisher's note to educators and parents: Our editors have carefully reviewed these web sites to ensure that they are suitable for children. Many web sites change frequently, however, and we cannot guarantee that a site's future contents will continue to meet our high standards of quality and educational value. Be advised that children should be closely supervised whenever they access the Internet.

Nota de la editorial a los padres y educadores: Nuestros editores han revisado con cuidado las páginas web para asegurarse de que son apropiadas para niños. Sin embargo, muchas páginas web cambian con frecuencia, y no podemos garantizar que sus contenidos futuros sigan conservando nuestros elevados estándares de calidad y de interés educativo. Tengan en cuenta que los niños deben ser supervisados atentamente siempre que accedan a Internet.

Index/Índice

About the Author

JoAnn Early Macken is the author of two rhyming picture books, *Sing-Along Song* and *Cats on Judy*, and more than 80 nonfiction books for children. Her poems have appeared in several children's magazines. She lives in Wisconsin with her husband and their two sons.

Información sobre la autora

JoAnn Early Macken ha escrito dos libros de rimas con ilustraciones, *Sing-Along Song* y *Cats on Judy*, y más de ochenta libros de no ficción para niños. Sus poemas han sido publicados en varias revistas infantiles. Vive en Wisconsin con su esposo y sus dos hijos.